11+
Verbal Reasoning
GL & Other Styles

WORKBOOK 2

Verbal Reasoning Technique

Dr Stephen C Curran

with Jacqui Turner

Edited by Andrea Richardson and Katrina MacKay

This book belongs to

ae
TUITION

Accelerated Education Publications Ltd

Contents

Chapter Five
LOGICAL REASONING

Logical Reasoning questions are of three types:
Tabular • **Relational** • **Positional**

1. Tabular Reasoning

These questions involve the processing of a large amount of information and are solved by creating a grid or table.

Example: Amandeep, Beth, Chris, Dhilan and Erin all play sports. Amandeep, Beth and Chris all play football. Dhilan plays rugby, netball and football. Amandeep plays tennis. Erin plays hockey and tennis. Beth plays rugby, netball and hockey.
a) Who plays the most sports?
b) Who plays the least sports?
c) Which child does not play rugby or football?

Set out the information on a grid like this. Make sure you have noted all the information from each of the statements.

	Football	Rugby	Netball	Tennis	Hockey
A	✓	✗	✗	✓	✗
B	✓	✓	✓	✗	✓
C	✓	✗	✗	✗	✗
D	✓	✓	✓	✗	✗
E	✗	✗	✗	✓	✓

Answers from the grid or table:
a) Beth plays the most sports. b) Chris plays the least sports. c) Erin does not play rugby or football.

Exercise 5: 1a   Answer the following:

1) Angela and Carole attend gym club. Craig likes chess and debating. Carole and Sue go to dance club on a Wednesday. Paul goes to football club and debating.

Complete the table from the above statements before answering the questions below:

	Gym	Chess	Debating	Dance	Football
Angela					
Carole					
Craig					
Sue					
Paul					

a) Which two students like debating? _____ & _____

b) How many children do two activities? _____

c) Which two activities does Carole do? _____ & _____

2) Five children earn money during the week. On Monday John and Matthew each earn £6. On Tuesday Philip gets £4 for washing the car and £6 for mowing the lawn on Friday. Jane babysits on Tuesday and earns £8. Katy and John deliver the local newspaper and earn £10 each on Friday.

	Mon	Tues	Wed	Thurs	Fri
John					
Matthew					
Philip					
Jane					
Katy					

a) Who earns the most money? _____

b) Which two people earn the same amount?

_____ and _____

c) On which day was most money earned? _____

3) Peter attended sports taster sessions for one week in the summer holidays. On Mondays and Wednesdays he did diving in the morning. He did rock climbing on Tuesday and Thursday. On Monday and Friday afternoon he did football. He did swimming on the same days as football. On Tuesday and Wednesday he did cycling.

	Mon	Tues	Wed	Thurs	Fri
Diving					
Rock Climbing					
Football					
Swimming					
Cycling					

a) On which day did he only do one activity? _____

b) Which was the busiest day? _____

c) On how many days did he do two activities? _____

4) The Shaw family went on a picnic. Jenny took a ham sandwich and an apple. Helen and Mum had cheese sandwiches. Mum had an orange and Helen took a banana. They all had orange juice to drink. Gran and Grandad had ham sandwiches. Gran had apple juice and Grandad had a cup of tea. Everyone except Mum had cake.

	Hm	Ch	Ap	Ba	Or	AJ	OJ	Tea	Ca
Jy									
Hn									
Mum									
Gran									
Grd									

a) Who had a ham sandwich, tea and cake? _____

b) How many things did Jenny eat and drink? _____

c) Who had fewest things to eat and drink? _____

Some questions require a much simpler grid, but it is still worth organising your ideas to avoid a mistake.

Example: There are five houses down a road. Only two houses have chimneys, one of which has a black front door and the other is red. Another two houses have porches and also have gardens. Some houses have trees in the front garden.

1. Place each item of information on a table using abbreviations.
2. Irrelevant information is often included.
3. Nothing is known about the fifth house. There is no mention of the features it may or may not have. The last statement about trees is irrelevant.

	Ch	Do	Po	Ga
1	✓	Bl		
2	✓	Re		
3			✓	✓
4			✓	✓
5				

The completely true statement must then be selected.

A. None of the houses has a yellow front door. **Unknown.**
B. None of the houses has a front gate. **Unknown.**
C. All of the houses have chimneys. **False.**
D. Those with chimneys also have gardens. **Unknown.**
E. **At least two of the houses have gardens. True.**

Exercise 5: 1b Answer the following:

5) During reading week at school Amir and Andrew chose non-fiction books. Spassia, Saskia and Cara chose fiction books. Saskia chose an adventure book. Amir chose a book on science and Spassia chose a story about horses. Cara read a book about dancing and Andrew read about space.

Complete the table from the above statements before answering the questions below:

	Type	About
Am		
An		
Sp		
Sa		
Ca		

Are the following statements **True**, **False** or **Unknown**?

A. Saskia chose a story about horses. _____

B. Amir wants to be a scientist when he grows up. _____

C. Cara read a fiction book about dancing. _____

6) At the shop Rose bought a chocolate bar and a cola for herself. Mark bought crisps and lemonade. Amrit had a chocolate bar and chocolate milk. Sian had some biscuits and chocolate milk. Suzie ate crisps and drank lemonade.

	Ate	Drank
Rose		
Mark		
Amrit		

Are the following statements **True**, **False** or **Unknown**?

A. Two people chose crisps and lemonade. _____

B. Rose does not like cola. _____

C. Suzie and Sian are sisters. _____

7) On the way to the theme park Sumit says that he wants to go on Thunder River and the Log Flume. Simran wants to go on the Banana Boat and the Roller Coaster. Their sister wants to go on the Tea Cups and the Sail Boats. Mum wants to go on the Log Flume and the Banana Boat.
Dad wants to go on the Roller Coaster and Thunder River.

	Choice 1	Choice 2
Sumit		
Simran		
Sister		
Mum		
Dad		

Are the following statements **True**, **False** or **Unknown**?
A. Mum is afraid of heights. _____
B. Dad and Sumit both want to go to Thunder River. _____
C. Mum and Simran want to go on the Banana Boat. _____

2. Relational Reasoning

Relational Reasoning questions appear in two forms:
Relative Information • **Relative Meaning**

A. Relative Information - This type involves sorting out and reordering statements that relate to each other.

Example:
> Bus 1 leaves the Bus Station at 11.15am. Bus 2 leaves at 10.45am. Bus 2 takes twice as long as Bus 3 to make the same journey. Bus 3 leaves 15 minutes after Bus 1 and arrives at 12.00pm.
>
> What time does Bus 2 arrive?
>
> A. 12.00pm   B. 11.45am
> C. 11.00am   D. 11.30am

It is important to understand each statement precisely and how it relates to the other statements. Reordering the statements will help unravel the information.

We need to find out about Bus 2. This is done by seeing how the timings for Bus 2 relate to the other buses. The information can be summarised as follows:

1. Bus 2 takes twice as long as Bus 3.
2. Bus 3 leaves 15 minutes after Bus 1, which means it leaves at 11.30am. (Bus 1 leaves at 11.15am.) It arrives at 12.00pm. It takes 30 minutes.
3. Bus 2 takes twice as long, so it takes 60 minutes to complete the journey.

Putting the information onto a chart can help. This can be done in a number of ways but below is a suggestion.

Bus 1	Bus 2	Bus 3
11.15am	10.45am	11.30am
	↓ Takes twice as long as Bus 3	↓ (30 mins)
Unknown	**11.45am**	12.00pm

Bus 2 left at 10.45am. The 60 minute journey means it arrives at 11.45am. Therefore the answer is B.

Exercise 5: 1c   Answer the following:

8) a) Three coaches take Year 5 on a school trip. Coaches A and C leave at 9.00am. Coach B leaves 15 minutes later because some people were late. Coach A does not stop and arrives at 10.30am. Coach B takes the same travelling time but stops for 15 minutes. Coach C stops for 30 minutes and takes 30 minutes longer because it got stuck in traffic.

Are the following statements **True**, **False** or **Unknown**?

A. Coach C arrived last. _____

B. Coach A stopped at the service station. _____

C. Coach B arrived at 11.00am. _____

b) Three children are making cakes in a cookery class. Child A makes 12 small cakes. They take 15 minutes to make and need to go into the oven for 20 minutes. Child B makes one large cake. It takes 20 minutes to make and has to bake for 35 minutes. Child C makes muffins. He takes 25 minutes to make them and bakes them for 25 minutes. Child A and B both start at 10.00am but child C is late for class and starts at 10.10am.

Are the following statements **True**, **False** or **Unknown**?

A. Child B's cake is ready 5 minutes before Child C's muffins. _____

B. Child A finishes first. _____

C. Child C got detention for being late. _____

B. Relative Meaning - Some questions involve selecting a statement from the possible answers that relates most closely to the meaning in the given statement. Example:

> ***Wolfgang Amadeus Mozart was very talented at music.***
> If this statement is true, only one of the sentences must be true. Which one?
> A. Wolfgang Amadeus Mozart played the piano.
> B. Wolfgang Amadeus Mozart loved to write music.
> C. Wolfgang Amadeus Mozart was a musician.
> D. Music is always performed by talented musicians.

Some possible answers may be true in themselves, but the correct answer must match the meaning of the given statement precisely and not add to or detract from it.

Answer A - 'Wolfgang Amadeus Mozart played the piano.' We are given no specific information about which instruments Mozart played.

Answer B - 'Wolfgang Amadeus Mozart loved to write music.' We are given no specific information about Mozart's attitude to music.

Answer D - 'Music is always performed by talented musicians.' It is not relevant to the statement and is not true.

Answer C - **'Wolfgang Amadeus Mozart was a musician.'**

This is the only answer that correctly matches the given statement in all respects. It follows that if *'Wolfgang Amadeus Mozart was very talented at music'*, he can be correctly called a musician.

Exercise 5: 1d Answer the following:

9) a) *Chimpanzees are primates. Chimpanzees are intelligent.*

Underline the only statement which must be true.

Chimpanzees are large.
Chimpanzees are clever and climb trees.
Chimpanzees are intelligent primates.

b) *Horses can jump fences. Horses can run fast.*

Underline the only statement which must be true.

Horses are the fastest animals.
Horses can run fast and jump fences.
Only horses can jump fences.

10) a) *Yachts are boats. Yachts have sails.*

Underline the only statement which must be true.

Yachts are sailing boats.
All boats are yachts.
All things with sails are yachts.

b) *Bicycles have wheels. Bicycles can be ridden.*

Underline the only statement which must be True.

Things with wheels are called bicycles.
Bicycles are ridden on roads.
Bicycles have wheels and can be ridden.

Record scores
out of ten here →

3. Positional Reasoning

Positional Reasoning questions appear in many forms. They can relate to **Age**, **Time**, **Direction**, **Size** and **Order**.

All positional reasoning questions are best solved with **diagrams**. This allows precise organisation of the given information and avoids confusion.

a. Basic Types

Most positional reasoning questions are straightforward and can be solved with a simple diagram.

Example:

In a block of flats, Simrat lives one floor above Carla and one floor below Kieran. Oliver lives two floors below Kieran. Which two people live on the same floor?
    A. Kieran and Oliver
    B. Carla and Simrat
    C. Carla and Oliver
    D. Simrat and Oliver
    E. Kieran and Simrat

Draw a grid that represents the floors of the block and, with trial and error, plot the position of each person.

3	K
2	S
1	C O

Eventually it will be seen there is only one possible combination that will fit all the requirements.

Answer: C. **Carla and Oliver** live on the same floor.

Exercise 5: 2a   Answer the following:

1) Christopher lives 5 miles away from his school and Steven lives two miles further away than Christopher. Anna lives 3 miles closer to the school than Steven. James lives 4 miles from the school.

_____

_____

_____

(Use these lines to plot their positions.)

Underline the answers. Are they **True**, **False** or **Unknown**?

A. Anna and James live the same distance from school.
   (True, False or Unknown)

B. Steven lives furthest from school.
   (True, False or Unknown)

C. Christopher lives 50 minutes away from school.
   (True, False or Unknown)

2) Four children walk their dogs in the park. Vijay walks for 40 minutes. Akash has a smaller dog so walks for 10 minutes less than Vijay. Priyanka walks for twice as long as Vijay. Craig takes his dog for a 45 minute walk. (Use the lines below to plot their positions.)

_____   _____   _____   _____

Underline the answers. Are they **True**, **False** or **Unknown**?

A. Priyanka walks for more than one hour.
   (True, False, Unknown)

B. Akash walks for half an hour. (True, False, Unknown)

C. Akash has the smallest dog. (True, False, Unknown)

3) There are four trees in a garden. The beech tree is twice as tall as the apple tree which is 4m high. The cherry tree is one and a half times the height of the apple tree. The oak tree is 12m high.

(Use the lines below to plot their positions.)

_____   _____   _____   _____

Underline the answers. Are they **True**, **False** or **Unknown**?

A. The oak tree is twice as high as the cherry tree.
(True, False or Unknown)

B. The apple tree and the cherry tree are the same height.
(True, False or Unknown)

C. The apple tree is half the height of the beech tree.
(True, False or Unknown)

---

4) In a donkey derby Ned finished two places behind Bella. Charlie was faster than Trudy but not as fast as Flossie. Bella finished just ahead of Trudy.

_____

_____

_____   (Use these lines to plot
                              their positions.)

_____

_____

Write whether the statements are **True**, **False** or **Unknown**?

A. Flossie was the fastest donkey. _____

B. Ned lost the race. _____

C. Trudy normally beats Bella. _____

b. Complex Types

Some positional reasoning questions are more **Complex**. They can still be solved with a diagrammatic approach, but it may not be quite so obvious which one to use.

Example: Sarah, Zoe, Max, Anya and Bridget are 6, 7, 7, 8 and 9 years old, but not in this order. Two of the children are twins. Sarah is two years younger than Anya. Zoe is two years younger than Max. Bridget is older than Sarah.
Which two children are twins?
> A. Sarah and Bridget
> B. Max and Anya
> C. Zoe and Sarah
> D. Bridget and Zoe
> E. Anya and Bridget

The information can be summarised as follows:

1. The five children are 9, 8, 7, 7 and 6 years old. The twins must be 7 years old. There is only a three year gap in age between all the children.

2. Sarah is two years younger than Anya.

3. Zoe is two years younger than Max.

4. Bridget is older than Sarah.

The statements must fit the pattern of the ages. Set out the ages and then try and fit the children into them.

The information provided in the first three statements only permits two possibilities as there are two year gaps in age between Sarah and Anya and between Zoe and Max.

Both possibilities are tested below in the age structure:

1st Possibility   (9) Anya
                           (8) Max
                           (7) Sarah   (7) Bridget
                           (6) Zoe

This is not the correct combination since the question states Bridget is older than Sarah (see statement 4).

2nd Possibility   (9) Max
                           (8) Anya
                           (7) **Zoe**   (7) **Bridget**
                           (6) Sarah

The only possible combination is: D.
Bridget and Zoe are twins.

Exercise 5: 2b   Answer the following:

5) a) In 2012 Felicity is two years old. Dillan is one year older than Jacob. Jacob is four years older than Miriam who was born in 2010. Holly is seven years younger than Dillan. _____

                                    _____   (Use the diagram
                                    _____   to help you.)

                                    _____

Underline the only statement that must be true.

A. Jacob is oldest.

B. Holly was born in 2010.

C. Felicity and Miriam are the same age.

b) If the day after tomorrow is Thursday, what day was it three days ago?   _____

(Use this diagram to help you.)   Today

_____   _____   _____   _____   _____   _____

4. Mixed Examples

Exercise 5: 2c Answer the following:

6) Anna has a black springer spaniel. Lara has two black and white cats. Judy has no pets. Katie has a black and white rat.

Underline the answers. Are they **True**, **False** or **Unknown**?

A. Judy does not like animals. (True, False, Unknown)
B. Lara has the most pets. (True, False, Unknown)
C. All of the pets have some black hair.
   (True, False, Unknown)
D. Anna has a dog. (True, False, Unknown)

---

7) a) *Rabbits have four legs. Rabbits have long ears.*

Underline the only statement which must be true.

Things with long ears are called rabbits.
Four-legged creatures are called rabbits.
Rabbits run fast because they have long legs.
Rabbits have long ears and four legs.

b) *Aeroplanes have wings. Aeroplanes fly.*

Underline the only statement which must be true.

Things which fly are called aeroplanes.
Birds have wings.
Aeroplanes fly using wings.
Things which have wings are called aeroplanes.

8) Daniel ran a race in 52 seconds. Steven ran it 5 seconds slower. Michael ran 7 seconds faster then Steven. The record for the race was 51 seconds.

Underline the only statement that must be True.

A. Daniel beat the record.

B. Steven ran faster than Daniel.

C. Steven and Daniel ran the race in the same time.

D. Michael beat the record.

9) Chris is four years older than Pauline, who is two years younger than Caroline. Caroline is 13 years old, six years older than Claire.

How old is Claire? (Underline the answer.)

A. Six years old

B. Seven years old

C. Eight years old

D. Nine years old

10) a) In two days time it will be Saturday. What day was it four days ago? (Underline the answer.)

A. Saturday

B. Sunday

C. Monday

D. Tuesday

b) It is five days until my birthday. If today is the 28th of June, what is the date of my birthday? (Underline the answer.)

A. The 31st of June

B. The 1st of July

C. The 2nd of July

D. The 3rd of July

Score

Chapter Six
MATHEMATICAL REASONING

There are four types of **Mathematical Reasoning** question:
Substitution • **Equation** • **Sequencing** • **Number Link**

1. Substitution

These questions employ a simple form of Algebra, where letters stand for numbers. **Substitute** the numbers for the letters and do the calculation (using $+ - \times \div$). When the answer is obtained it must be converted back to a letter.

Example:

$A = 2, B = 3, C = 4, D = 6, E = 12$
What is the answer to this sum written as a letter?

Substitute the numbers for the letters:

$A \times B + D$

$2 \times 3 + 6 = 12$ (E)

The answer is: **E**

Exercise 6: 1 Write the answer as a letter:

Score

1) $A = 1, B = 2, C = 3, D = 4, E = 6$
What is the answer to this sum written as a letter?

$A + B + C = \underline{\quad\quad}$

2) **A = 3, B = 4, C = 7, D = 8, E = 10**

What is the answer to this sum written as a letter?

$$D - C + A = \underline{\qquad}$$

3) **A = 4, B = 6, C = 11, D = 16, E = 20**

What is the answer to this sum written as a letter?

$$E \div A + B = \underline{\qquad}$$

4) **A = 2, B = 5, C = 8, D = 10, E = 15**

What is the answer to this sum written as a letter?

$$E - C - B = \underline{\qquad}$$

5) **A = 6, B = 8, C = 12, D = 16, E = 20**

What is the answer to this sum written as a letter?

$$D \div B \times A = \underline{\qquad}$$

6) **A = 3, B = 4, C = 7, D = 20, E = 40**

What is the answer to this sum written as a letter?

$$D \times B - E = \underline{\qquad}$$

7) **A = 9, B = 12, C = 15, D = 18, E = 21**

What is the answer to this sum written as a letter?

$$B + C - A = \underline{\qquad}$$

8) **A = 2, B = 5, C = 7, D = 11, E = 24**

What is the answer to this sum written as a letter?

$$C \times B - D = \underline{\qquad}$$

9) $A = 4, B = 5, C = 9, D = 16, E = 20$

What is the answer to this sum written as a letter?

$$D \div A + B = \underline{\qquad}$$

10) $A = 3, B = 7, C = 12, D = 16, E = 21$

What is the answer to this sum written as a letter?

$$A + D - C = \underline{\qquad}$$

2. Arithmetic Equations

It is important to understand the relationship between the Four Rules of Number. **Inverse** means **Opposite**.

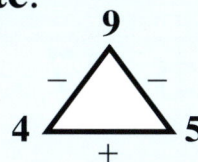

+ and − are a pair of operations.

$5 + 4 = \mathbf{9};$ $9 - 4 = \mathbf{5};$ $9 - 5 = \mathbf{4}$

× and ÷ are a pair of operations.

$3 \times 4 = \mathbf{12};$ $12 \div 4 = \mathbf{3};$ $12 \div 3 = \mathbf{4}$

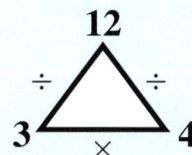

Equations are mathematical sentences. The numbers on the left side are **Balanced**, or **Equal**, to what is on the right side. This is signified by an **Equals Sign**.

The Equals Sign means a missing number can be found. **Inverse Operations** can be used to solve the equations.

Remember: + is **inverse to** − and × is **inverse to** ÷

Example: | Find the missing number in this equation:
$$7 \times 6 = 210 \div [?]$$

1. Multiply 7×6

$$7 \times 6 = 210 \div [?]$$

2. To find the dividing number a division is necessary.

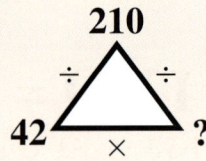

$$42 = 210 \div [?]$$

$$42 = 210 \div \boxed{5}$$

$$42 = 42$$

Divide $210 \div 42 = 5$

The answer is: **5**

Exercise 6: 2   Find the missing number:

1) $6 + 15 = 29 - [?]$ _____

2) $17 - 4 = 13 \times [?]$ _____

3) $14 + [?] = 15 \times 2$ _____

4) $81 \div [?] = 3 \times 3$ _____

5) $3 + 39 = 7 \times [?]$ _____

6) $13 \times 3 = 27 + [?]$ _____

7) $144 \div [?] = 6 \times 2$ _____

8) $109 - 37 = 9 \times [?]$ _____

9) $16 \times 4 = 49 + [?]$ _____

10) $11 \times 11 = 60 + [?]$ _____

Score

3. Number Sequencing

The Four Rules of Number are the basis for all **Number Sequence** operations. $+ \; - \; \times \; \div$

Adding and **Subtracting** types could be called 'slow' sequences as the numbers get bigger or smaller slowly.

Multiplying and **Dividing** types could be called 'fast' sequences as the numbers get bigger or smaller quickly.

a. Adding and Subtracting
(i) Basic Sequences

Basic Adding and Subtracting Sequences comprise:

1. Arithmetic Progressions
(Add/subtract a constant number)

$$\overset{+2}{3,} \; \overset{+2}{5,} \; \overset{+2}{7,} \; \overset{+2}{9,} \; \overset{+2}{11,} \; \overset{+2}{13,} \; ?$$

Example 1:

Add **2** to the previous number.

The next number will be: **15**

2. Increasing or Decreasing Gaps
(Add/subtract an increasing or decreasing number)

$$\overset{+1}{1,} \; \overset{+2}{2,} \; \overset{+3}{4,} \; \overset{+4}{7,} \; \overset{+5}{11,} \; \overset{+6}{16,} \; ?$$

Example 2:

Add **1**, then add **2**, then add **3**, etc.

The next number will be: **22**

3. Alternating Gaps
(Add/subtract numbers on an alternating basis)

$$\overset{+7}{1,} \; \overset{-3}{8,} \; \overset{+6}{5,} \; \overset{-4}{11,} \; \overset{+5}{7,} \; \overset{-5}{12,} \; ?$$

Example 3:

Add **7**, subtract **3**, add **6**, subtract **4**, etc.

The next number will be: **7**

Exercise 6: 3   Find the missing number:

1) 2, 5, 8, 11, 14, _____

2) 36, 31, 26, 21, 16, _____

3) 27, 28, 30, 33, 37, _____

4) 2, 3, 6, 7, 10, _____

5) 79, 74, 70, 67, 65, _____

6) 27, 41, 55, 69, 83, _____

7) 3, 10, 7, 13, 9, _____

8) 101, 108, 115, 122, 129, _____

9) 209, 201, 194, 188, 183, _____

10) 63, 53, 44, 36, 29, _____

b. Multiplying and Dividing

Earlier features also apply to Multiply and Divide sequences.

Basic Multiplying and Dividing Sequences comprise:

1. Multiply or Divide by the same number
(Multiply/divide repeatedly)

$$\underset{\times 2}{\quad}\ \underset{\times 2}{\quad}\ \underset{\times 2}{\quad}\ \underset{\times 2}{\quad}\ \underset{\times 2}{\quad}\ \underset{\times 2}{\quad}$$
1, 2, 4, 8, 16, 32, ?

Example 1:

| Multiply by **2** on a repeated basis. |

The next number will be: **64**

This can also be seen as an arithmetic increasing gap sequence:
1, +1 2, +2 4, +4 8, +8 16, +16 32, +32 64, etc.

24   © 2012 Stephen Curran **ae**

2. Geometric Progressions
(Multiply/divide repeatedly by an increasing number)

$\times 2 \quad \times 3 \quad \times 4 \quad \times 5 \quad \times 6$

1, 2, 6, 24, 120, ?

Example 2:

> Multiply by **2**, then by **3**, then by **4**, etc.

The next number will be: **720**

3a. Multiplying the Gaps
(Multiply/divide the gap by the same number)

$(2 \times 2) \quad (4 \times 2) \quad (8 \times 2) \quad (16 \times 2)$
$+2 \quad +4 \quad +8 \quad +16 \quad +32$

0, 2, 6, 14, 30, ?

Example 3a:

> Multiply the gap by **2** repeatedly, etc.

The next number will be: **62**

The sequence can be explained as a Double Operation:

3b. Double Operations
(Two operations, e.g. multiply, then subtract for the next number)

$(\times 2 + 2), (\times 2 + 2), (\times 2 + 2), (\times 2 + 2), (\times 2 + 2)$

0, 2, 6, 14, 30, ?

Example 3b:

> Multiply by **2**, then add **2**, etc.

The next number will be: **62**

Exercise 6: 4   Find the missing number:

Score

1) **4, 8, 16, 32, 64, _____**

2) **2,187, 729, 243, 81, 27, _____**

3) **6, 12, 36, 144, 720, _____**

4) **7, 9, 13, 21, 37, _____**

5) **20,160, 2,880, 480, 96, 24, _____**

6) **28,672, 7,168, 1,792, 448, 112, _____**

7) **2, 3, 6, 15, 42, _____**

8) **4, 12, 36, 108, 324, _____**

9) **15,625, 3,125, 625, 125, 25, _____**

10) **1, 1, 2, 6, 24, _____**

c. Mixed Examples

Exercise 6: 5   Find the missing number:

1) **20, 40, 80, 160, 320, _____**

2) **9, 10, 12, 15, 19, _____**

3) **1, 5, 13, 29, 61, _____**

4) **99, 67, 51 43, 39, _____**

5) **22, 25, 30, 33, 38, _____**

6) **8, 8, 9, 11, 14, _____**

7) **30,000, 3,000, 300, 30, 3, _____**

8) **3, 12, 30, 66, 138, _____**

9) **4, 6, 9, 13, 15, _____**

10) **50, 52, 47, 50, 46, _____**

4. Number Links

The Four Rules of Number are the basis for all **Number Link** questions: $+ \quad - \quad \times \quad \div$

There are two types of number link question:

Single Operation • **Double Operation**

a. Single Operation

Single Operation number link questions involve performing one mathematical calculation $(+ \quad - \quad \times \quad \div)$ on two numbers to produce a linking third number.

Example: Find the missing number:

(12 [24] 2) **(14 [56] 4)**
(16 [?] 6)

Identify the operation; multiply in this example.

$$\overset{\times}{\frown}$$ **(12 [24] 2)** $\overset{\times}{\frown}$ **(14 [56] 4)**

Multiply **16 × 6 = 96** $\overset{\times}{\frown}$ **(16 [96] 6)**

Exercise 6: 6 Find the missing number:

Score

1) **(6 [48] 8)** **(7 [63] 9)**
(2 [?] 7)

_____

2) (64 [47] 17)   (72 [43] 29)
   (102 [?] 84)   _____

3) (28 [42] 14)   (37 [56] 19)
   (19 [?] 62)   _____

4) (72 [9] 8)   (35 [5] 7)
   (42 [?] 6)   _____

5) (16 [48] 3)   (21 [105] 5)
   (13 [?] 6)   _____

6) (12 [25] 13)   (19 [33] 14)
   (24 [?] 17)   _____

7) (121 [11] 11)   (140 [35] 4)
   (160 [?] 8)   _____

8) (227 [96] 131)   (340 [179] 161)
   (420 [?] 83)   _____

9) **(6 [8] 48)**   **(12 [11] 132)**

       (9 [?] 126)   _____

10) **(7 [56] 8)**   **(6 [48] 8)**

       (8 [?] 9)   _____

b. Double Operations

Double Operation number link questions involve performing two mathematical calculations (+ − × ÷) to produce the linking third number.

1. Type 1 - Linear Calculations

Example: | Find the missing number:

(2 [10] 50)   **(5 [25] 125)**
     (4 [?] 100)

Identify the operation that is used twice in this example.

$$\times 5 \quad \times 5$$
(2 [10] 50)   **(5 [25] 125)**
$$\times 5 \quad \times 5$$

$$\times 5 \quad \times 5$$
(4 [20] 100)

Multiply **4 × 5 = 20 × 5 = 100**

Exercise 6: 7   Find the missing number:

Score

1) **(4 [8] 16)**   **(5 [10] 20)**
     (3 [?] 12)   _____

2) (8 [13] 18)   (1 [6] 11)

       (5 [?] 15)   _____

3) (64 [16] 4)   (32 [8] 2)

       (48 [?] 3)   _____

4) (22 [15] 8)   (50 [43] 36)

       (35 [?] 21)   _____

5) (11 [33] 99)   (4 [12] 36)

       (6 [?] 54)   _____

6) (15 [28] 41)   (54 [67] 80)

       (32 [?] 58)   _____

7) (144 [24] 4)   (180 [30] 5)

       (36 [?] 1)   _____

8) (96 [75] 54)   (63 [42] 21)

       (71 [?] 29)   _____

9) **(2 [18] 162)**   **(5 [45] 405)**

            (4 [?] 324)   ———

10) **(294 [42] 6)**   **(196 [28] 4)**

          (245 [?] 5)   ———

2. Type 2 - Basic then Sporadic Calculations

First Calculation: A **Basic Calculation** ($+ - \times \div$) following the same pattern as a Single Operation question between the two given numbers.

Second Calculation: A **Sporadic** and **Unrelated** **Calculation** ($+ - \times \div$) not specifically connected to the given numbers.

(i) First Calculation - Adding or Subtracting

Example: | Find the missing number:

(15 [36] 3)   **(17 [42] 4)**

        (12 [?] 2)

First Calculation: Check whether there has been an add, subtract, multiply or divide between the two numbers. There has been an **addition** in this example.

(15 [36] 3)   **(17 [42] 4)**

$15 + 3 = 18$ $17 + 4 = 21$

(12 [?] 2) $12 + 2 =$ **14**

Second Calculation: This calculation is not related to the given numbers, so it has to be spotted by examining the number relationships.

Trial and Error: It can only be one of four operations; adding, subtracting, multiplying or dividing by an unknown number. In this case it is **multiply by 2**.

(15 [36] 3) 15 + 3 = 18   (17 [42] 4) 17 + 4 = 21

Second Calculation 18 × 2 = 36   Second Calculation 21 × 2 = 42

(12 [?] 2) First Calculation 12 + 2 = 14

Second Calculation

14 × 2 = 28 **(12 [28] 24)**

Exercise 6: 8 Find the missing number:

Score

1) **(21 [80] 19)**   **(53 [134] 14)**
   (49 [?] 23)   _____

2) **(63 [27] 54)**   **(41 [12] 37)**
   (33 [?] 26)   _____

3) **(36 [70] 104)**   **(74 [45] 16)**
   (92 [?] 28)   _____

4) **(87 [43] 42)**   **(24 [8] 14)**
   (48 [?] 27)   _____

5) **(21 [15] 16)**   **(46 [33] 35)**
   (13 [?] 10)   _____

6) **(34 [20] 6)**   **(57 [35] 13)**
   (22 [?] 8)   _____

7) **(65 [30] 45)**   **(24 [26] 8)**
   (42 [?] 16)   _____

8) **(42 [12] 36)**   **(34 [30] 19)**
   (63 [?] 59)   _____

9) **(32 [73] 45)**   **(24 [36] 16)**
   (62 [?] 20)   _____

10) **(63 [9] 27)**   **(39 [5] 11)**
   (82 [?] 28)   _____

(ii) First Calculation - Multiplying or Dividing

Example: | Find the missing number:

$$(40\ [15]\ 2) \qquad (36\ [7]\ 3)$$
$$(24\ [\ ?\ ]\ 4)$$

First Calculation: Either × or ÷. This time it is a division between the two numbers.

$$\overset{\div}{(40\ [15]\ 2)} \qquad \overset{\div}{(36\ [7]\ 3)}$$

$$40 \div 2 = 20 \qquad 36 \div 3 = 12$$

$$\overset{\div}{(24\ [\ ?\ ]\ 4)} \quad 24 \div 4 = \boxed{6}$$

Second Calculation: The second unrelated calculation arising from the number relationships is **subtract 5**.

(40 [15] 2) 40 ÷ 2 = 20   (36 [7] 3) 36 ÷ 3 = 12

Second Calculation 20 − 5 = 15   Second Calculation 12 − 5 = 7

(24 [?] 4)   First Calculation 24 ÷ 4 = 6

Second Calculation

$$6 - 5 = \boxed{1} \qquad (24\ [1]\ 4)$$

Exercise 6: 9   Find the missing number:

Score

1) $(60\ [16]\ 10) \qquad (25\ [15]\ 5)$
$$(42\ [\ ?\ ]\ 6)$$

2) **(8 [26] 3)**   **(13 [28] 2)**
   (7 [?] 4) _____

3) **(10 [27] 2)**   **(3 [31] 8)**
   (5 [?] 6) _____

4) **(24 [2] 6)**   **(45 [3] 9)**
   (56 [?] 8) _____

5) **(7 [18] 3)**   **(2 [9] 6)**
   (8 [?] 4) _____

6) **(45 [15] 9)**   **(16 [14] 4)**
   (24 [?] 6) _____

7) **(2 [15] 7)**   **(5 [31] 6)**
   (4 [?] 4) _____

8) **(3 [6] 3)**   **(15 [27] 2)**
   (8 [?] 6) _____

9) **(16 [8] 4)**   **(72 [12] 9)**
          (42 [?] 6)   _____

10) **(10 [45] 4)**   **(17 [39] 2)**
          (50 [?] 5)   _____

5. Mixed Examples

Score

Exercise 6: 10   Answer the following:

1) a) **A = 0, B = 3, C = 6, D = 7, E = 11**
   What is the answer to this sum written as a letter?

   $$C \times B - D - E = \underline{\quad}$$

   b) **A = 2, B = 6, C = 8, D = 9, E = 12**
   What is the answer to this sum written as a letter?

   $$C \times D \div E = \underline{\quad}$$

2) a) **A = 2, B = 7, C = 8, D = 16, E = 30**
   What is the answer to this sum written as a letter?

   $$E \div A - C = \underline{\quad}$$

   b) **A = 3, B = 8, C = 15, D = 24, E = 72**
   What is the answer to this sum written as a letter?

   $$E \div B \div A = \underline{\quad}$$

3) a) $A = 2, B = 6, C = 12, D = 18, E = 36$

What is the answer to this sum written as a letter?

$$D \times A \div B + C = \underline{\hspace{1.5cm}}$$

b) $A = 3, B = 4, C = 15, D = 72, E = 144$

What is the answer to this sum written as a letter?

$$E \div A \div B + A = \underline{\hspace{1.5cm}}$$

4) a) $3 \times 15 = 90 \div [?]$ $\underline{\hspace{1.5cm}}$

b) $144 \div 72 = 8 - [?]$ $\underline{\hspace{1.5cm}}$

c) $201 + 169 = 37 \times [?]$ $\underline{\hspace{1.5cm}}$

5) a) $2012 \div 4 = 450 + [?]$ $\underline{\hspace{1.5cm}}$

b) $16 \times 8 = 4 \times [?]$ $\underline{\hspace{1.5cm}}$

c) $96 + [?] = 13 \times 8$ $\underline{\hspace{1.5cm}}$

6) a) $961 - [?] = 2012 - 1954$ $\underline{\hspace{1.5cm}}$

b) $16 \times 4 = 128 \div [?]$ $\underline{\hspace{1.5cm}}$

c) $52 + [?] = 11 \times 13$ $\underline{\hspace{1.5cm}}$

7) a) $28, \ 26, \ 23, \ 19, \ 14, \ \underline{\hspace{1.5cm}}$

b) $6, \ 42, \ 252, \ 1{,}260, \ 5{,}040, \ \underline{\hspace{1.5cm}}$

c) $7, \ 8, \ 9, \ 11, \ 13, \ \underline{\hspace{1.5cm}}$

8) a) **6, 30, 150, 750, 3,750,** _____

b) **998, 989, 980, 971, 962,** _____

c) **29, 42, 55, 68, 81,** _____

---

9) a) **(16 [13] 3)   (8 [1] 7)**
   (9 [?] 4)   _____

b) **(30 [6] 5)   (81 [9] 9)**
   (64 [?] 4)   _____

c) **(4 [12] 36)   (7 [21] 63)**
   (5 [?] 45)   _____

10) a) **(6 [34] 4)   (3 [25] 5)**
    (7 [?] 2)   _____

b) **(9 [12] 6)   (12 [32] 4)**
   (25 [?] 15)   _____

c) **(56 [4] 7)   (240 [8] 20)**
   (125 [?] 25)   _____

Chapter Seven
REVISION
1. Letter Sequencing

A B C D E F G H I J K L M N O P Q R S T U V W X Y Z

Exercise 7: 1a Write the missing letters:

1) PZ QY RX SW ____

2) AB GH BC HI ____

3) ZB VD RF NH ____

4) LP MQ OS RV ____

5) FV GU IS LP ____

2. Alphabet Codes

Exercise 7: 1b Write the missing letter or letters:

6) FH is to IE as NP is to ? ____

7) If the code for CAR is BYO, what is the code for RAW? ____

8) If the code for SAW is UXA, what is the code for NOT? ____

9) If NZO stands for SET, what does KVI stand for? ____

10) If the code for TRY is NMU, what does CHL stand for? ____

Score

3. One Word Patterns

Exercise 7: 2a Fill in the missing word:

1) (spam   maps)   (room   moor)
        (liar   ?)   _____

2) (plant   tall)   (psalm   mass)
        (sling   ?)   _____

3) (sling   gins)   (slant   tans)
        (slits   ?)   _____

4) (plaid   paid)   (grave   gave)
        (snore   ?)   _____

5) (sinks   skin)   (carts   star)
        (gowns   ?)   _____

4. Two Word Patterns

Exercise 7: 2b Fill in the missing word:

6) (hand [stand] stamp)   (give [_____] prone)

7) (dare [grade] grand)   (late [_____] stall)

8) (deck [check] chest)   (cast [_____] blame)

9) (core [chore] short)   (peat [_____] clean)

10) (pour [colour] cloud)   (arms [_____] gales)

5. Secret Codes

Exercise 7: 3a Find the answers to the following:

Match these number codes to the correct words:

TRAPS	PARTS	SPORT	STRAP
54632	41325	52314	23145

1) Find the code for the word **PORTS**. _____

2) What word has the code **52132**? _____

3) Find the code for the word **STOAT**. _____

Match these number codes to the correct words:

GRAVE	VASE	SAVE	EAGER
21524	6132	54132	3162

4) Find the code for the word **SAGE**. _____

5) What word has the code **52146**? _____

6. Letter Shifts

Exercise 7: 3b Answer the following:

6) **PLANT** and **SAND**   become _____ and _____

7) **GRAVE** and **PAWN**   become _____ and _____

8) **AMENDS** and **LENT** become _____ and _____

9) **VOICE** and **SON**   become _____ and _____

10) **PROWL** and **SICK**   become _____ and _____

7. Compound Words

Exercise 7: 4a Write the compound word:

1) (chest head neck)
   (let nut not)

   _____

2) (par slow next)
   (slay ting now)

   _____

3) (bar tar star)
   (lest link fish)

   _____

4) (out part play)
   (in mean side)

   _____

5) (mail hill mill)
   (top stop sort)

   _____

8. Hidden Words

Exercise 7: 4b Write the hidden four-letter word:

6) This temporary job will finish at Christmas.

   _____

7) However you write an addition the answer
   is the same. _____

8) This year will be amazing. _____

9) He has great earning ability because of
   his qualifications. _____

10) The values on both sides were equal so
    the sum balanced. _____

Score

9. Missing Letters

Exercise 7: 5a Fill in the missing letter:

1) **gra** [?] **urst**
   sta [?] **orrow**

   The letter is ____ .

2) **singl** [?] **asy**
   ambl [?] **arn**

   The letter is ____ .

3) **stra** [?] **arts**
   glo [?] **orry**

   The letter is ____ .

4) **stin** [?] **ing**
   pin [?] **ettle**

   The letter is ____ .

5) **powe** [?] **estore**
   laye [?] **elay**

   The letter is ____ .

10. Analogies

Exercise 7: 5b Underline the word that will complete the analogy:

Score

6) **Heavy** is to **light** as **soft** is to (gentle, hard, easy)

7) **Absent** is to **away** as **present** is to (hear, gift, here)

8) **Music** is to **notes** as **words** is to (books, letters, notes)

9) **Change** is to **alter** as **stay** is to (remain, remind, stop)

10) **Hair** is to **hare** as **their** is to (them, there, hare)

11. Similar Meanings

Exercise 7: 6a Underline the two words closest in meaning:

1) (close   king   pen)   (inch   ruler   lord)

2) (perhaps   bright   power)   (might   same   slower)

3) (glow   dim   dome)   (slow   shine   bright)

4) (stay   vehicle   transport)   (car   remove   stop)

5) (transparent   opaque   solid)   (visible   slight   clear)

12. Word Links

Exercise 7: 6b Underline the word link for the word pairs:

6) (weak   powerless)   (flimsy   frail)

   (poor, slim, feeble, faint, sorry)

7) (drip   seep)   (tell   reveal)

   (link, spill, slip, leak, call)

8) (meaning   spot)   (aim   object)

   (point, print, thing, place, stop)

9) (undress   uncover)   (band   ribbon)

   (reveal, revel, real, strap, strip)

10) (rapid   swift)   (hasty   abrupt)

   (quickly, short, quick, ploy, sudden)

Score

          ae

13. Opposite Meanings

Exercise 7: 7a Write the words most opposite in meaning:

1) (forward back change)
   (onward reverse stop)

   _____ _____

2) (highest raise risk)
   (lower least rose)

   _____ _____

3) (scare please praise)
   (score scold scald)

   _____ _____

4) (simple complete conflict)
   (able easy complex)

   _____ _____

5) (dear cheap sharp)
   (expensive slope solid)

   _____ _____

14. Odd Ones Out

Exercise 7: 7b Write the odd ones out:

6) diary, magazine, journal, log, letter

   _____ _____

7) piece, peace, part, port, portion

   _____ _____

8) celebrity, celebration, party, star, gathering

   _____ _____

9) plane, plain, basic, steady, simple

   _____ _____

10) gown, garment, dress, grown, cloth

   _____ _____

Score

15. Missing Words

Exercise 7: 8a What is the missing three-letter word?

1) Please **AL** John to attend the party.

   The five possibilities are:
   NOT NOW LOW SOW TEN _____

2) He swam the width of the pool **BE** the water.

   The five possibilities are:
   SET LOW LET FOR NOT _____

3) I like crumpets with lots of **TER**.

   The five possibilities are:
   NOT BET SET BUT LET _____

4) He had a good view of the **DIST** hills.

   The five possibilities are:
   LET SET NET TAN TEN _____

5) The windows were covered in **GE**.

   The five possibilities are:
   NOW ROW RAT RIM RAM _____

16. Logical Reasoning

Exercise 7: 8b   Answer the following:

6) On Mondays, Mrs Jones teaches Years 7, 8, 9 and 10. Mr Watson has Years 13, 10 and 12. Mrs Holmes has Years 9, 11 and 12. Mrs Mills only teaches Years 12 and 13.

   (Clue: draw a table to help you)

   a) Which teacher teaches most year groups? _____

   b) How many teachers have Year 12 on a Monday? _____

   c) How many Year 12 and 13 lessons are there? _____

7) Some children have been saving their pocket money for 7 weeks. James saved £3 a week. Peter had a total of £15. Grace had £5 more than James. Ruth had £10 already and then saved £2 a week. Anna had £30 but then spent £12 on a present for her mum.

   a) Who had the most money? _____

   b) Who had the least money? _____

8) *A lending library loans books. There are many types of books in the library.*

   Underline the only statement which must be True.

   A building with books is called a library.
   There are only a few types of books in a library.
   You can buy books in a library.
   You can borrow many types of books from a library.
   You can keep books that you borrow.

9) Chris is facing north-east. He turns anticlockwise through three right angles. Which way is he facing now? _____

   A. North-west
   B. South-west
   C. South-east
   D. North-east

   N
   W ← ┼ → E
   S

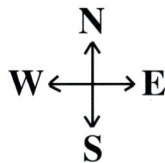

10) Yesterday was Sunday. How many days is it until Friday? _____

Score

17. Substitution

Exercise 7: 9a Write the answer as a letter:

1) $A = 2$, $B = 4$, $C = 8$, $D = 12$, $E = 64$
   What is the answer to this sum written as a letter?

   $E \div B \div A =$ _____

2) $A = 13$, $B = 15$, $C = 17$, $D = 22$, $E = 24$
   What is the answer to this sum written as a letter?

   $E + A - B =$ _____

3) $A = 2$, $B = 6$, $C = 7$, $D = 17$, $E = 57$
   What is the answer to this sum written as a letter?

   $B \times C + D - A =$ _____

4) $A = 2$, $B = 12$, $C = 17$, $D = 18$, $E = 40$
   What is the answer to this sum written as a letter?

   $C \times A + D - B =$ _____

5) $A = 12$, $B = 18$, $C = 20$, $D = 31$, $E = 84$
   What is the answer to this sum written as a letter?

   $E \div A + D - B =$ _____

18. Arithmetic Equations

Exercise 7: 9b Find the missing number:

6) $13 \times 4 = 36 + [?]$ _____

7) $84 \div 4 = 7 \times [?]$ _____

8) $117 - [?] = 7 \times 8$ _____

9) $20 + 40 = 12 \times [?]$ _____

10) $12 + 29 = 44 - [?]$ _____

Score

19. Number Sequencing

Exercise 7: 10a Find the missing number:

1) 3, 7, 13, 21, 31, _____

2) 36, 33, 30, 27, 24, _____

3) 17, 12, 23, 18, 29, _____

4) 75, 69, 64, 60, 57, _____

5) 3, 21, 147, 1,029, 7,203, _____

20. Number Links

Exercise 7: 10b Find the missing number:

6) (12 [60] 5)   (16 [64] 4)

   (6 [?] 9)   _____

7) (63 [74] 11)   (83 [95] 12)

   (58 [?] 13)   _____

8) (448 [56] 7)   (192 [24] 3)

   (320 [?] 5)   _____

9) (13 [25] 37)   (96 [65] 34)

   (22 [?] 68)   _____

10) (12 [67] 6)   (3 [19] 8)

    (11 [?] 9)   _____

Notes

Answers

Chapter Five
Logical Reasoning

Exercise 5: 1a

1) a) Craig and Paul
   b) 3
   c) Gym and Dance
2) a) John
   b) Philip and Katy
   c) Friday
3) a) Thursday
   b) Monday
   c) 3
4) a) Grandad
   b) 4
   c) Mum

Exercise 5: 1b

5) A. False
   B. Unknown
   C. True
6) A. True
   B. False
   C. Unknown
7) A. Unknown
   B. True
   C. True

Exercise 5: 1c

8) a) A. True
      B. False
      C. True
8) b) A. True
      B. True
      C. Unknown

Exercise 5: 1d

9) a) Chimpanzees are intelligent primates.
   b) Horses can run fast and jump fences.
10) a) Yachts are sailing boats.
    b) Bicycles have wheels and can be ridden.

Exercise 5: 2a

1) A. True
   B. True
   C. Unknown
2) A. True
   B. True
   C. Unknown
3) A. True
   B. False
   C. True
4) A. True
   B. True
   C. Unknown

Exercise 5: 2b

5) a) C. Felicity and Miriam are the same age.
   b) Saturday

Exercise 5: 2c

6) A. Unknown
   B. True
   C. True
   D. True
7) a) Rabbits have long ears and four legs.
   b) Aeroplanes fly using wings.
8) D. Michael beat the record.
9) B. Seven years old
10) a) B. Sunday
    b) D. The 3rd of July

Chapter Six
Mathematical Reasoning

Exercise 6: 1

1) E
2) B
3) C
4) A
5) C

Answers

6) E
7) D
8) E
9) C
10) B

Exercise 6: 2
1) 8   2) 1
3) 16   4) 9
5) 6   6) 12
7) 12   8) 8
9) 15   10) 61

Exercise 6: 3
1) 17
2) 11
3) 42
4) 11
5) 64
6) 97
7) 14
8) 136
9) 179
10) 23

Exercise 6: 4
1) 128
2) 9
3) 4,320
4) 69
5) 8
6) 28
7) 123
8) 972
9) 5
10) 120

Exercise 6: 5
1) 640
2) 24
3) 125
4) 37
5) 41
6) 18
7) 0.3
8) 282
9) 18
10) 50

Exercise 6: 6
1) 14   2) 18
3) 81   4) 7
5) 78   6) 41
7) 20   8) 337
9) 14   10) 72

Exercise 6: 7
1) 6   2) 10
3) 12   4) 28
5) 18   6) 45
7) 6   8) 50
9) 36   10) 35

Exercise 6: 8
1) 144   2) 21
3) 60   4) 19
5) 9   6) 15
7) 36   8) 8
9) 78   10) 11

Exercise 6: 9
1) 17   2) 30
3) 37   4) 5
5) 29   6) 14
7) 17   8) 45
9) 11   10) 255

Answers

Exercise 6: 10

1) a) A
   b) B
2) a) B
   b) A
3) a) D
   b) C
4) a) 2
   b) 6
   c) 10
5) a) 53
   b) 32
   c) 8
6) a) 903
   b) 2
   c) 91
7) a) 8
   b) 15,120
   c) 16
8) a) 18,750
   b) 953
   c) 94
9) a) 5
   b) 16
   c) 15
10) a) 24
    b) 40
    c) 1

Chapter Seven
Revision
Exercise 7: 1a

1) TV
2) CD
3) JJ
4) VZ
5) PL

Exercise 7: 1b

6) QM
7) QYT
8) PLX
9) PAN
10) IMP

Exercise 7: 2a

1) rail
2) gill
3) sits
4) sore
5) snow

Exercise 7: 2b

6) prove
7) stale
8) blast
9) pleat
10) glares

Exercise 7: 3a

1) 46325
2) START
3) 52612
4) 6152
5) GEARS

Exercise 7: 3b

6) plan and stand (t)
7) gave and prawn (r)
8) mends and leant (a)
9) vice and soon (o)
10) prow and slick (l)

Exercise 7: 4a

1) chestnut
2) parting
3) starfish
4) outside
5) hilltop

Answers

Exercise 7: 4b
6) stem 7) very
8) beam 9) tear
10) also

Exercise 7: 5a
1) b 2) e
3) w 4) k
5) r

Exercise 7: 5b
6) hard 7) here
8) letters 9) remain
10) there

Exercise 7: 6a
1) king, ruler
2) power, might
3) glow, shine
4) vehicle, car
5) transparent, clear

Exercise 7: 6b
6) feeble
7) leak
8) point
9) strip
10) sudden

Exercise 7: 7a
1) forward, reverse
2) raise, lower
3) praise, scold
4) simple, complex
5) cheap, expensive

Exercise 7: 7b
6) magazine & letter
7) peace & port
8) celebrity & star
9) plane & steady
10) grown & cloth

Exercise 7: 8a
1) LOW
2) LOW
3) BUT
4) TAN
5) RIM

Exercise 7: 8b
6) a) Mrs Jones
   b) 3
   c) 5
7) a) Grace
   b) Peter
8) You can borrow many types of books from a library
9) C. South-east
10) Four

Exercise 7: 9a
1) C 2) D
3) E 4) E
5) C

Exercise 7: 9b
6) 16 7) 3
8) 61 9) 5
10) 3

Exercise 7: 10a
1) 43
2) 21
3) 24
4) 55
5) 50,421

Exercise 7: 10b
6) 54
7) 71
8) 40
9) 45
10) 94

PROGRESS CHARTS

Shade in your score for each exercise on the graph. Add up for your total score. An adult will work out the percentage.

5. LOGICAL REASONING

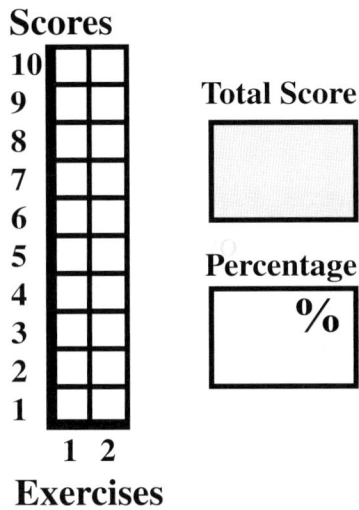

Scores

10		
9		
8		
7		
6		
5		
4		
3		
2		
1		

1 2

Exercises

Total Score

Percentage
%

6. MATHEMATICAL REASONING

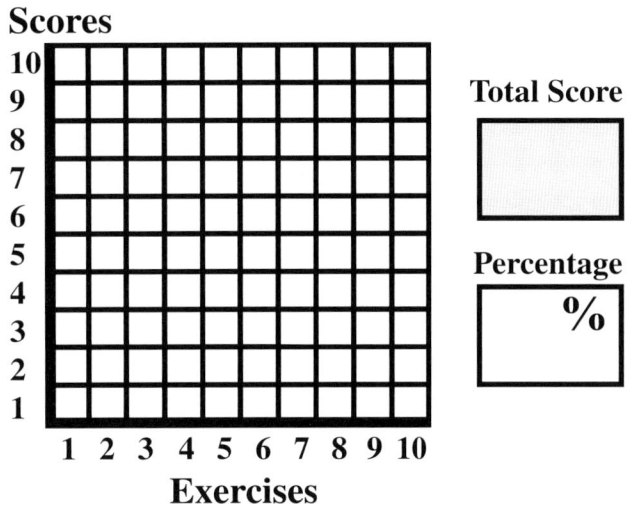

Scores

1 2 3 4 5 6 7 8 9 10

Exercises

Total Score

Percentage
%

7. REVISION

Scores

1 2 3 4 5 6 7 8 9 10

Exercises

Total Score

Percentage
%

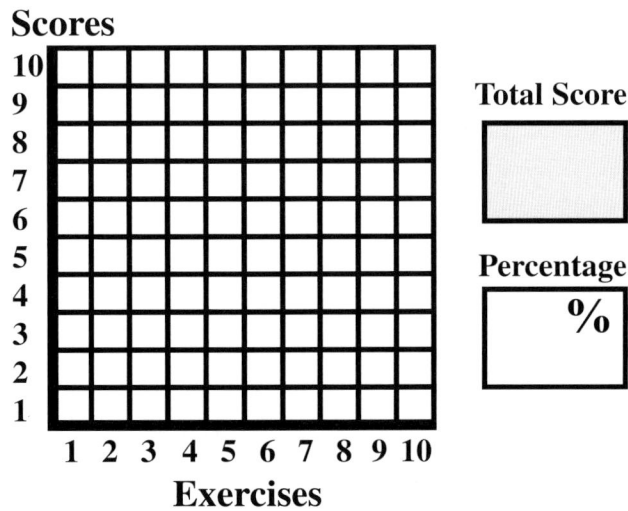

Add up the percentages and divide by 3

Overall Percentage

%

CERTIFICATE OF

ACHIEVEMENT

This certifies

_____

has successfully completed

11+ Verbal Reasoning
Year 4/5 GL & Other Styles

WORKBOOK **2**

Overall percentage
score achieved

%

Comment _____

_____

Signed _____
(teacher/parent/guardian)

Date _____